SURVIVAL ZONE

SURVIVE A HURRICANE

BY PATRICK PERISH

TORQUE™

BELLWETHER MEDIA · MINNEAPOLIS, MN

TM

Are you ready to take it to the extreme? Torque books thrust you into the action-packed world of sports, vehicles, mystery, and adventure. These books may include dirt, smoke, fire, and chilling tales. **WARNING** : read at your own risk.

This edition first published in 2017 by Bellwether Media, Inc.

No part of this publication may be reproduced in whole or in part without written permission of the publisher. For information regarding permission, write to Bellwether Media, Inc., Attention: Permissions Department, 5357 Penn Avenue South, Minneapolis, MN 55419.

Library of Congress Cataloging-in-Publication Data

Names: Perish, Patrick, author.
Title: Survive a Hurricane / by Patrick Perish.
Description: Minneapolis, MN : Bellwether Media, Inc., [2017] | Series:
   Torque: Survival Zone | Includes bibliographical references and index. |
   Audience: 007-012.
Identifiers: LCCN 2015049957 | ISBN 9781626174436 (hardcover : alk.
paper)
Subjects: LCSH: Hurricanes–Juvenile literature. | Severe storms–Juvenile
   literature.
Classification: LCC QC944.2 .P48 2017 | DDC 613.6/9–dc23
LC record available at https://lccn.loc.gov/2015049957

Printed in the United States of America, North Mankato, MN.

TABLE OF CONTENTS

HOWL OF THE HURRICANE

On the eve of September 16, 2004, Michielle Beck and her daughter sat, worried, inside their Florida home. They knew Hurricane Ivan would make **landfall** that night.

The wind got louder. Michielle's dogs felt the pressure drop and began to whine. She stepped out back to see the storm. Powerful winds pushed her and whipped rain against her face. Back inside, the power blinked and went out.

"The wind had begun to [...] shriek. It sounded like a woman screaming."
-Michielle Beck

"It sounded like the roof was just going to leave at any minute."
-Michielle Beck

Michielle and her daughter slept on a blanket in the bathroom. They could feel the house shake from heavy **gusts**.

YOU NAME IT

Hurricanes are named from an alphabetical list, starting each year with A. Hurricane Ivan was the ninth named storm in 2004.

The next morning, they saw the destruction Ivan had left. Roofs were torn off. Downed telephone poles blocked roads. Some houses were completely swept away. But Michielle and her daughter were safe!

HOW HURRICANES HAPPEN

Hurricanes are one of the most dangerous forces on the planet. They begin as thunderstorms over **tropical** ocean waters. As they move, they pick up warm, moist air and grow larger. Then their wind speed increases, and they begin to rotate.

Meteorologists track hurricanes as they move over the ocean. They warn people about when and where they think a storm will hit.

PARTS OF A HURRICANE

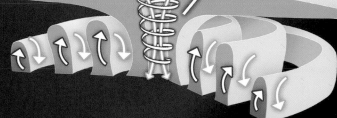

eye   eyewall

— cold air sinking

— hot air rising

TOPSY-TURVY

Hurricanes that form in the northern part of the world spin counterclockwise. Those that form in the south spin clockwise. This is because of Earth's rotation.

SURVIVING NATURE'S FURY

The best way to survive a hurricane is to plan ahead. Make an **evacuation** plan. Pack supplies before the storm arrives.

EMERGENCY KIT LIST

 flashlight

 extra batteries

 first aid kit

 emergency radio

 candles

 matches

 dry or canned food

 bottled water

 clothing

 sleeping bags

 pillows

 road maps

 medications

 cell phone and charger

Listen to weather reports for orders to leave. Families in **mobile homes**, tall apartments, or coastal homes should evacuate. If you must evacuate, leave early. Heavy traffic can cause delays.

TOP OFF

Be sure to fill the car's gas tank before an evacuation is ordered. Gas stations may be closed or have long lines once evacuation begins.

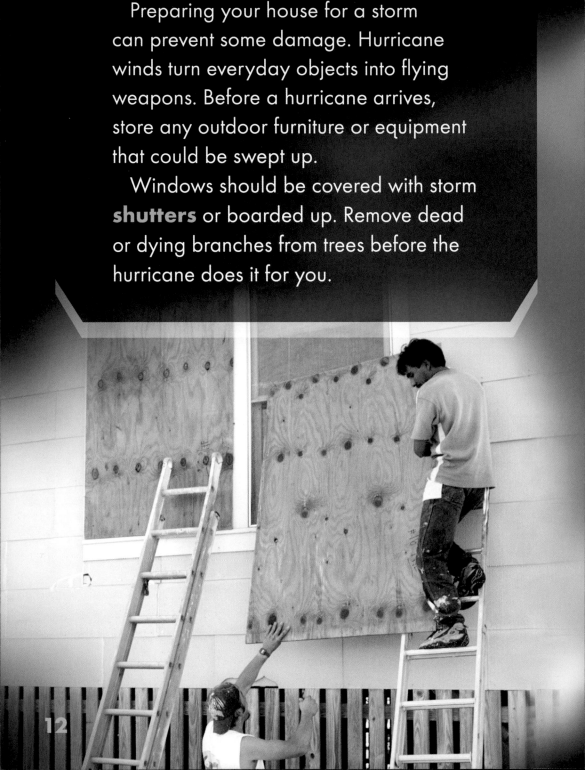

Preparing your house for a storm can prevent some damage. Hurricane winds turn everyday objects into flying weapons. Before a hurricane arrives, store any outdoor furniture or equipment that could be swept up.

Windows should be covered with storm **shutters** or boarded up. Remove dead or dying branches from trees before the hurricane does it for you.

HURRICANE WIND SCALE

In the Saffir-Simpson hurricane wind scale, hurricanes are categorized by their continuous wind speed.

CATEGORY 1:
74 - 95 mph (119 - 153 km/h)

- roofs damaged
- shingles ripped off
- large tree branches snapped off

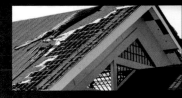

CATEGORY 2:
96 - 110 mph (154 - 177 km/h)

- major damage to roofs and sidings
- small trees uprooted or snapped
- power outage likely

CATEGORY 3:
111 - 129 mph (178 - 208 km/h)

- roofs ripped off
- many trees uprooted and broken
- no power or clean water for days
  or weeks

CATEGORY 4:
130 - 156 mph (209 - 251 km/h)

- extreme damage to roofs and walls
- most trees snapped or uprooted
- area unlivable for weeks to months

CATEGORY 5:
157+ mph (252+ km/h)

- many homes destroyed
- downed power lines
- area unlivable for weeks to months

If you are waiting out the storm, stay inside away from windows. Listen to weather reports for updates.

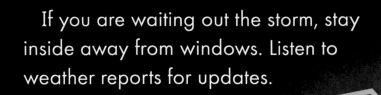

safe room after storm

SAFETY FIRST

Some families add safe rooms to their houses. These strong shelters protect against high winds and flying debris.

eye

Wait for the all clear before going outside. Do not be fooled by the sudden calm of the **eye**. When it passes over, winds briefly die down. But soon the other side of the storm hits.

Hurricane winds drive huge amounts of water onto the shore. This rising of waters is called a **storm surge**.

GODLY STORMS

The word "hurricane" comes from Huracán, a Caribbean storm god.

Prepare for flooding if you live near the coast. Move things off the floor to prevent flood damage. If you have a basement, move any valuables to a higher place.

AFTER THE STORM

After a hurricane leaves the ocean, it grows weaker. But not before bringing heavy rains. This can cause severe flooding. Avoid floodwaters. They may hide downed power lines or fast-moving water.

Flooding can mix **sewage** or harmful chemicals into the drinking water. Do not drink water from the sink until authorities say it is safe.

Even after the storm, there are dangers. People may be trapped in their homes. **Power outages** can last for days. Damaged buildings may crumble without warning. Avoid downed power lines and watch out for broken glass and other **debris**.

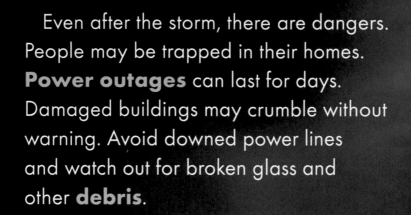

MANY NAMES

In the Indian Ocean, hurricanes are called cyclones. In the western Pacific Ocean, they are typhoons. Their scientific name is tropical cyclones.

Hurricanes can be deadly. But your chance of survival can increase. Prepare well and stay safe during and after a hurricane!

GLOSSARY

debris—the remains of something broken down or destroyed

evacuation—the process of leaving a dangerous area

eye—the low-pressure center of a hurricane

gusts—bursts of wind

landfall—the arrival of a hurricane on land

meteorologists—scientists who study and predict the weather

mobile homes—trailers that are used as houses at a permanent site

power outages—losses of electricity to an area

sewage—human waste and waste water

shutters—outside coverings for windows

storm surge—the rise of water levels caused by powerful winds during a hurricane

tropical—part of the tropics; the tropics is a hot, rainy region near the equator.

AT THE LIBRARY

Challoner, Jack. *Eyewitness Hurricane & Tornado*. New York, N.Y.: DK Publishing, 2014.

Gregory, Josh. *The Superstorm Hurricane Sandy*. New York, N.Y.: Children's Press, 2013.

Raum, Elizabeth. *Surviving Hurricanes*. Chicago, Ill.: Raintree, 2012.

ON THE WEB

Learning more about surviving in a hurricane is as easy as 1, 2, 3.

1. Go to www.factsurfer.com.

2. Enter "survive a hurricane" into the search box.

3. Click the "Surf" button and you will see a list of related web sites.

With factsurfer.com, finding more information is just a click away.

INDEX